On the Beach
with Chet Baker

Also by Robert Seatter:
Travelling to the Fish Orchards

ROBERT SEATTER

On the Beach with Chet Baker

seren

Seren is the book imprint of
Poetry Wales Press Ltd
57 Nolton Street, Bridgend, Wales, CF31 3AE
www.seren-books.com

The right of Robert Seatter to be identified as
the Author of this Work has been asserted in accordance
with the Copyright, Designs and Patents Act, 1988.

ISBN 978-1-85411-428-0

A CIP record for this title is available from the British Library.

The publisher acknowledges the financial assistance
of the Welsh Books Council.

Cover photograph: UrbanImage.tv/Gerry Bahl

Printed in Hoefler by the Cromwell Press Ltd, Trowbridge

Contents

10 poems, beginning and ending in a garden

A story has no beginning or end: arbitrarily one chooses that moment of experience from which to look back or from which to look ahead.
– The End of the Affair, Graham Greene

I COME FROM

I come from a suburb waiting forever
for the train to London,
from smashed windows, graffiti,
fog on the platform,
skinheads and fights
if you look the wrong way
I come from clean handkerchiefs,
dinner money, God,
please and *sorry* one hundred times over,
draft excluders and double glazing
I come from *Chambers Etymological Dictionary*,
maths tables, 11+, *Look & Learn*,
an almost complete set of *Observer I-spy* books,
from a family of teachers and yet more teachers,
an Orkney grandfather, a Shropshire grandma,
from no accent at all
I come from kindness
I come from doh-re-me: *The Sound of Music*,
recorders, clarinets, a pianola
all the way from Scotland
I come from sin and masturbation,
rats behind the garage,
and a man who followed me
back from the library
I come from silence
I come from a garden
from my father mowing the lawn into the dark,
from fences, walls, gates and hedges,
Cuthberts seed packets, *The Perfect Small Garden*,
from the sound through the night
of trains, trains, trains

TORTOISE

For my father

That bright yellow flash – a road stripe
on lacquer – glared on his shell.

We daubed it there for his own good
when he got old; he *would* wander off,

get lost in the leaves, seep into mud,
seem clogged, almost given up.

Seeing it, we would scoop him up
in our small, kind hands, out of the ditch,

feel his head and legs slamming back inside:
the shutting of the lid on an ancient box.

We would set him to be watched
where every shadow marked him,

every bevelled claw, every silent step
against the sunlight's glare,

where our trail of yellow lettuce leaves
remained untouched across the lawn,

as he began his journey back
towards the dark, leaving words like stones:

I want to be sleeping in this last house of my own.
Paint me no longer into your light.

SIXTEEN

It rained caterpillars all that summer,
down from the apple tree, the cracked tarpaulin
of the old shed roof,
worn-out August sky –

thick, brown, wriggly rain
that bounced as it fell,
sprawled on our windowsills,
the runnels of a dustbin lid,
table and chairs left out in the garden;

invaded the house,
inched along our toothbrushes on their polished
glass shelf, dangled
in the airing cupboard – a slow uncurling,

waited in our pockets, our unlaced shoes,
trouser legs, shirt arms,
a trail of odd socks, the edges of a poster
unsticking from the wall

till at night, we heard them
marking the rooms,
twitching hairs, munching, munching –

as if our house might slowly
fall apart,
brick and plaster, screw and nail,
and we'd wake to a morning
of empty air,
then at last on our faces
real, wet rain.

MASKS

As if we were all waiting – seconds, days, years –
to be somebody else, and it just took this city
to tip us over the edge into nothing left of ourselves
but eyes. We all succumb: the giggling American student,
the nurse from Turin gone white-faced, implacable,
a bank manager from Bordeaux eating ravioli
through a face full of feathers, the macho Argentinian
turned camp and peacock, a Spanish girl
with a single butterfly eye, glittering antenna into her hairline.
Arlechino, Cat Woman, a blue-haired clown,
Mickey Mouse, the Ice Queen, the face of Primavera.
In this city, what you choose is what you seem –
simple as that. And now here we are, crushed
without ceremony into Venice McDonalds.
Colombina is pushing a ketchuped burger
into her papier maché face. Batman is twisting
his Coca-Cola straw under a cardboard hood.
We are mixed up and muddled on the mirror walls;
we are making too much noise.
Now you have, in front of you, my plain white face –
anonymous, floating – like something you might watch
on the bottom of a river. Now I have the sound of you,
but muffled and inward, a voice inside a box inside a box
inside a box, and sometimes there are tricks –
acoustic reflections off the too-close walls:
you are Mickey Mouse, you are Batman,
you are the blue-haired clown.
Even at night when we take off our masks, leave them
watching us there on the dressing table,
we mistrust the faces we find: wait for the next one,
the next one after that, kiss hard and strong –
as if we would bite right through to the teeth, the bone.

THE DRAGON OF LOVE

After the painting by Alekos Fassianos, 1983

In the picture, the blue man with windy hair
is pedalling a bicycle,
while attempting to hold
what looks like a bad-tempered red cat
under his left arm.

The blue man is pedalling.
The wind is blowing.
The red cat is struggling.
It all looks a terrible effort,
which feels right, quite right –

trying to keep that damn bicycle going,
while you're grappling with a feeling
that may be bigger
than all the bicycles, the roads, the days
you ever knew,

which may in fact be the red dragon of love.
On the other hand,
you may have it all wrong, quite wrong.
It may be just
a spiteful red cat.

WHISPERING GALLERY

Our hands are around the inner dome
as if we are holding up its circle of space,
glitter of mosaic high above our heads

like a million buttons doing, undoing light.
My legs feel weak, I cannot look down.
Yet I have to do this, else, why the climb,

the wasted minutes? Now my lips are here
against the wall, and I'm whispering
the way that everyone does *Can you hear me?*

Can you hear me? I'm willing my message
to come out the way I want, neck at an angle,
ear towards the wall, and for you to hear it

as something like the same, then repeat it
across the space. *Can you hear me?*
Can you hear me? We keep on doing this

till our voices come scurrying back,
out of the dark, out of the glitter
asking us if we heard what we thought we said.

COMPUTER

I am past the hammer through the glass phase,
a nightmare of green writing on the back of my eyeball
or twitch of knuckle, finger joints.

Have grown to almost like it now:
its secret box of light,
its library of sounds that populates my day.

Can even take a Mr Neat satisfaction
in my tidy row of files
like monogrammed handkerchiefs out on a washing line
or my gliding mouse which vanishes text
and magicks it up somewhere else, eternally proving trust.

I might even stretch to a strange affection
for the way it takes my untidy thoughts –
tube ticket epigrams, backs of envelope scrawl –
and turns them into a paper tongue
with perfect type in Albertina, Garamond, New Times Roman,
the occasional exoticism of Matisse ITC.

Or the one-off moments it gives me
like this morning's email direct from France,
labelled *Subject: Amour*, telling me my body has become
'abstracted' which I take to mean portable, constant,
something that is always with you,

which only needs the click of an *on* button
for your fingers to touch me, lightly so lightly.

ON THE BEACH WITH CHET BAKER

I like the way that Chet rhymes *glove* with *love,*
and occasionally almost makes the notes fit,
wavering just the attractive side of flat

and going slow, slow, slow into the song.
It's good on my Walkman
here our last day lying on this Greek beach.

I can hear the waves behind it,
especially when he pauses for breath,
reaches for his trumpet

and they come scuttling in, shushing against the beat.
Then a water skier whirrs across the horizon,
a group of Italian tourists pauses at the curving balustrade

down to the beach, has a noisy conversation,
then straggles on along the cliff.
And distracted from Chet

I lie suddenly here in an English autumn,
leaves up to my ankles, cold city mornings, the turning year
turning again. I am starting lists, suspending them

across a going-grey sky.
And you and I, we are living in gaps,
departing from the meanings we didn't quite manage,

but getting by. This is good, I tell myself,
Chet would approve. We are *getting lost,*
which Chet rhymes with *defrost.*

We are turning this black Greek night
which we scrapped and cried in
into presence and absence, some sort of together.

But now Chet is back again
with the long, breathful pauses of *My Funny Valentine,*
and *my favourite work of art* which he rhymes with *heart*

and all the mystery of trying to make the big
and the little things fit
seems just like the breath, the precarious breath

of Chet's halting voice
and the way his trumpet comes
suddenly from nowhere, high exalted

then leaves a little gap for the shush of the waves
to run up the beach and down again,
up and down again.

CLARINET

I wanted to be Acker Bilk –
Stranger on the Shore. My aspiration.

But all those years of once-a-week lessons,
I could never make you sing.
I squeaked and puffed.
Never made it past the effortful stage.
I hated you

for not giving me a voice, for making
my fingers stick on your keys,
for splitting your reeds and swallowing
my breath, for the way you allowed my sister
to say – *Oh stop it, for heavens sake!*
This is how you do it. For the song

I could never catch
out there on the beach in a long, grey wavy line
with its specks of seagull, its crash of water
moving under my feet.
For not letting me be

that somebody else – the waited for
or the one who waits.

AMSTERDAM

You are telling me what you have just eaten –
six courses, *all small portions* you say in a tone of excusing,
and the meal began with a bottle of red,

ended with one of white.
Your words down the phone from Amsterdam
are a series of shiny white plates

oozing prawns and pancakes, Indonesian sattees,
some strange piece of beef, and Dutch apple cake
with a generous quiff of vanilla ice cream.

I can see them quite precisely those shiny white plates,
spinning in the dark from Amsterdam to London.
There is the trace of your tongue, your breath,

a fingerprint there on the curve of a rim.
There is your characteristic gesture as you lean
from the table, satisfied, smiling, pushing the plate away,

and there is the unknowability of you
heaped under wine, aroma, tiredness,
lying long-limbed next to the canals of Amsterdam.

There is your night and my night, in which after all
we do not touch. But those floating white plates
are a sort of comfort. The words, the parts of you

that come from here to there, the ways you find
to say what you cannot say,
the darkness which is not so dark after all.

MAGNET

The red and black magnet came in a Christmas kit.
Discover the world of science's attractions it said on the pack.
There was a face too, which you made from metal filings
on a shiny grey board – gave it a beard or a moustache,
the long, thin sideburns of an exotic pirate,

while the eyes stared and stared, fixed, unlidded, indifferent.
Strange how many times I've seen those eyes,
and the faces I made up at ten or eleven; how many times
I've gone right through to the hard grey board,
then recomposed a face again, plucked a beard from a crowd,

pair of eyebrows, a foreign moustache, kissed and passed,
kissed and passed. And now here I am examining your sideburns,
fine black hairs moving to a point in the middle of your cheek.
I stare at them as you sleep through morning,
head on the pillow. I would not move a single filing.

POSTCARDS FROM PORTUGAL

I've been writing postcards to you all week,
and not sent one of them.
I've been talking to you too –

like the madman in Praça de Rossio,
or the boy on the train shouting the words
of the George Michael song on his Walkman.

He looks very bookish, an all-A student,
not the type who'd keep saying
I want your sex.

By the time I get off, it's Celine Dion:
the love theme from *Titanic,*
and he's singing to someone, no-one,

that his love will go on and on.
I make a mental note,
write you another postcard.

THE ROUGH GUIDE TO PORTUGUESE

The consonants are at least consistent:
c *is soft before* e *and* i, *hard otherwise –*
unless it has a cedilla – acucar *(sugar)*
is pronounced 'assookar'. I will need that
for your three spoons in coffee;
in your black tea maybe it is even four.
And I will learn perhaps to find consistency
a surprise, or not to search for it.
J *is pronounced like the* s *in pleasure.*
This is Sunday afternoon's half light
through the bedroom blinds. I am practising
slow *ss* to remember them later.
The vowels are worse – flat and truncated,
they're often difficult for English-speaking tongues
to get round. Is it this that appeals?
I am in your mouth for a moment. I catch you
fleetingly on the tip of my tongue.
I cannot make you stay. *When two vowels*
come together, they continue to be enunciated
separately, except in the case of ei *and* ou.
I will rub against you till we blur a little.
I will be separate and one. But the memory
will elude me at the next word, and I am back
where I started. *More common is* ao,
which sounds something like a strangled yelp
of 'ow', *cut off in mid-stream, as in* pao –
bread, sao – *saint,* limao – *lemon.*
A saint of bread and lemons,
what can I do with such a bitter saint?
Even if you speak no Portuguese at all,
there are a few key words which can help you out.
Do you speak English? (Fala ingles?)
and I don't understand (Nao compreendo).
But how much will you understand when I say
I don't understand, when I make the strangled cry
cut off in mid-stream, when I pray in the dark
to a saint of bread and bitter lemons?

PAST INTERROGATIVE

Did you went? he says when tired,
wrestling with English grammar
out of his native Portuguese
or the French he speaks at work on the phone.
I blink at the mistake, thrown back
into a double past, his and mine;
one door slamming and then another.

Or else we're walking steps out of sync
in parallel roads (one of which
just might be the road where he lives).
A colour of a door, a loop of curtain –
we'll recognise something soon we say –
our feet walk with that hope.

Now a tree that burns in a mad autumn red
at a connecting street corner (*that's it,*
we say), where we'll stop and meet ourselves,
know how we came there – his past,
my past – and perhaps how we go on.

ON NOT RECEIVNG
A BIRTHDAY CARD FROM YOU

Your writing was nothing like mine.
Your waving *ts* and *hs*, italicised *es* like half-open eyes,
as looped back upon themselves – a profile through a scarf,
head turning into that fine mesh of wool.

I am thinking of it now – in November, my birthday month,
when there always came a card from you.
Splashed with mermaids, henna-red hair, your colour.
That was the last one.

Or something Pre-Raphaelite – your extravagant taste
never thrown over: *King Cophetua and the Beggar Maid,*
Hylas with the Nymphs. All your white skin too,
and the intricate tendrils of flowers and lamps
like your writing across and through those cards.

Your fingers always curled themselves into spaces –
the handles of tiny coffee cups, white almost see-through;
around an eccentric umbrella handle; squeezed into
tight black gloves – in days when students never wore gloves.

You twisted your words too, in the notes you wrote me
when you were eighteen, twenty-eight, lost in your thirties.
Writing that coiled up tight,
then undid itself in wilder, flyaway *ys* and *gs,*
set those descenders racing to the bottom of the page.

As if you had finally said all those things
you would never have to answer for –
turned mermaid, dived into open water, a flash of white,
a long trail of fin, then gone.

THE OBLONG MIRROR

I'm a stranger here myself... Kurt Weill/Ogden Nash

Come back tomorrow for fresh fish, they tell me,
when I ask for sausages.

*Pay us for the watch, the six half-made suits,
that topiary tree* when I'm after an umbrella,
a stout pair of walking shoes.

I haven't felt so tearful since I was six years old,
when my mother's blue skirt vanished through a line
of long, tree legs, and I counted pavement squares
till I'd used up all my numbers.

I keep hoping I might recognise the door I came out of,
face on a billboard, a road sign name,

when I suddenly see a man who looks just like me
standing in the middle of this city square,
confident, concentrated, with an eye to his wristwatch.

I see him again in a pub's oblong mirror –
his head thrown backwards, laughing loudly,
as if he really understands the punchline of the joke.

I watch him intently, wondering how he does it.
It looks so easy being me.

Now I hear him talking behind me on the bus:
it's his version of the story of a day in my life,
with a topiary tree, a dog-tooth check,
a soft grey Italian flannel.

At the next stop, I think, I'll turn round and ask him
how he does me so well,

and what he has done with that coatless man,
caught under a storm cloud,
on his way, he thought, to somewhere else.

PHOTOBOOTH

the six of us bundled into Paul's green Mini
like we were trying to compete with that ad
for how many people you can get in a Mini plus the elephant
and Hilary singing all the songs from *Cabaret*
kicking her legs so we all bounced up and down
and everyone's arms and legs turning into someone else's
and the windows steamed up against the night cold
more songs more more – *Life is a cabaret*
Maybe this time we squeal the top notes
Money makes the world go round...
and Paul driving like a maniac out past Richmond Windsor
till the roads got emptier and emptier
and when Hilary stopped singing we could hear
the planes overhead and see the streaks of the red tail lights
and all of us shouting out of the windows
Liz's long hair streaming backwards against her face
then Paul zigzagging from terminal
to terminal and no-one really knowing what to do
and why we were there and all of us feeling
more and more out of it because after all
the point of coming to an airport is to go somewhere else
and we had nowhere to go – it was a night out
in London it was the end of college
it was speeding somewhere nowhere and holding that moment
against the bigness of all those planes in the sky
then someone had the idea of the photobooth
the six of us piling into it being stupid being sad
trying to catch everything in that space of concentration
when we counted 1-2-3-4-5 seconds
and the green light flashed and then Jen
putting in another 50p piece and breathing
against the camera glass because she wanted to hold that too
then Paul driving us back to London
Hilary and Frank waving the sticky strips against the wind
till they flapped back and stuck against the car window
and there were our faces outside laughing back at us
and all of us never ever meeting again
though I can still see our faces so clearly

feel the heat of us close inside that car
hear the planes roaring overhead as we fell
out of that photobooth blinking and blinking

LOOKING FOR THE ROCKING HORSES

You are giving me directions, carefully,
for I always lose myself here – where every village
looks the same to me: little grey boxes, rained-on
slate roofs, an enterprising slap of ugly pebbledash,
the one Spar shop, predictable. *Past the campsite* you say,
and I bundle your small son into my car, swerve off
with instinct. But now it is serious, for I feel his nervousness
here at my side. He imagines, I know, the worst scenario –
every one sold, the shop under an earthquake,
yesterday's conversation of orders and presents all made up,
that even the roads may lose themselves,
the village turn into puddles and clouds. So we'll never arrive,
will become a part of that world of lost things:
one wheel off a toy yellow tractor, Spiderman's cape,
grandma, grandpa, the neighbour's tortoiseshell cat.
How much time? and *How much time more?* he asks.
I can only give him those weak adult words *Almost there*.
But we are past the campsite, now left at the postbox –
he is craning his neck, he is ready with the door.
For this is everything he's wanted. Then we round the corner
and suddenly see them, waiting in a row
on the pavement before us, prancing foreign
in this small, grey street. Heads high, lifted,
nosing different air, they jostle their browns, their blacks,
their reds, all their fluidity caught in the moment.
There's something in their glass eyes that seems so familiar,
simple as a marble – yet quite unknowable;
something in their manes so groomed and flat
that calls for the pull, the tangle of wind;
and something in their legs splayed wide on rockers
that's just where we wanted them – yet wants the space
of never being here. *When can we let it go?* he says,
as we haul the huge shape in corrugated cardboard into the car,
something unmanageable inside our arms.
And all the way home I hear it, like him,
knocking and knocking its blind, parcelled head
against the car rear window.

ANGEL IN THE RAMBLAS, BARCELONA

Charlie Chaplin had the look just right
a yard of pavement down the street:
his baggy trousers, his unreliable bendy cane.

And Dracula coming out of his coffin
with musical effects and bloodied teeth
made the most of his moment,
had the Spanish kids screaming.

Even Christopher Columbus on his two-foot column,
finger pointing out to America,
was given gravitas by city dust.

But the Angel in the Ramblas
was out of place and worse –

feathery white wings tied badly to his back,
shift and socks grubbily grey,
a grey face too, a cap of off-white string hair.

He stood there for hours –
an unbelievable statue
who couldn't quite get the pose right.

But in spite of it all, this angel spoke to us.
Stuck on his box among the exhaust fumes,
flightless, speechless, miming benediction,
he stopped traffic and hearts.

And we missed his presence
when we walked back down the street,
peered in vain among the birds and roses
for his off-white shape above the crowds.

Charlie was off on another twirling caper.
Dracula was rising fresh-fanged from his box.
But our tawdry angel had packed up and gone,

leaving us only with what we almost were –
our stuttering gestures, inarticulate words,
our impulses checked, so almost-kind.

I WILL BUY YOU CHOCOLATES

Song for Jacques Brel

Something in the burnt-out edge of the voice –
a texture of brown which says I once was green.
I began back there and now I am here,

in a raincoat, inside a steamed-up café,
watching the slow, slow circle of a brandy glass,
my hands that stick to the cheap formica.

Or coming out of the doors of a cinema,
eyes unsettled by bright afternoon –
three o'clock? three thirty?

Is it still the same old city?
And all that story merely a fiction
which drops behind me into the dark.

I bought you chocolates – Belgian, best –
but find the moment has passed me by.
A major or minor miscalculation:

the wrong face or the wrong pair of shoes?
Today, I should have been brilliant, funny,
instead I am only maladroit;

the celebration of all those wrong moments,
all that tender love which bruises the hand,
the *I never meant to say this/what I meant was that,*

the *don't go away* which turns into *go, just go.*
And I'm back here in the circle of my brandy glass –
though I still raise my glass to you and you,

and all the others who have trouble not believing.
I am bruised but uncynical.
I will buy you chocolates – Belgian, best.

MESSAGE FROM ELVIS

Elvis Costello is singing
Almost Blue on the kitchen radio.
And outside in the garden, rain.

My radio speakers keep cutting out –
perhaps it's the weather. *Almost* –

Almost he sings. Then *Blue* –
Blue. A fine white line between the words.

This is what I want – a room full of you, blue.
This is what I have – a crackle of speakers, rain,
the space to you or the you I thought you'd be.

I hear all the words of the song,
but I only hear *Almost.*
I hear only *Almost,*
I hear all the words of the song.

SNOW

The first of the year, and there are whoops of excitement
inside the office, as we desert our PC screens,
watch its slow motion,

turning and turning in the five o'clock air.
Down on the street, cars drag heavy hoods on their backs,
pedestrians are snowmen, soft-armed, beleaguered.

No sound comes up to us, in our world of too warm –
we laugh at a silent film from behind the picture window,
at the gesture that waits for a caption somewhere else.

Like the way your arm, your trusting arm,
comes reaching out for me sometimes in the dark.
How little is the space, how large the feeling,

which touches us gently after, like snowfall.
And we lie there waiting for the snow to come again,
believing it will and not quite believing.

ON FLYING TO MEET YOUR NEW LOVER

It's the nervousness of planes,
humming in the night – somewhere
over France, somewhere over Spain;
a trusting to pilots with antennae

through glass and messages for comfort.
It's a cloud behind a cloud, becoming
a mountain, as I lose my music
on the in-flight system, turn one song

to another, confuse all the languages:
hear Russian as Italian, English as Spanish.
It's cities below me, covered in silence –
when I know there's noise: a shout,

a whisper, a kiss for a beginning, words
you carry forever in your head, those rows
of books that mutter in the night and faces laughing
loudly out of photographs, the sound

of gesture. It's my ears blocking up, a part of me
falling below the plane's engines, presence
that turns into something else. It's now as the glass door
parts to make us meet, so I have the print of him,

can no longer ever imagine. It's his name
wearing a white shirt and a black suede jacket.
It's drinking coffee – the three of us now, our faces
in the bar mirror. The taste of the difference.

COUNTING

From that other city, you are moving towards me,
closing the door with the merest of clicks,

yet I can hear it – summer, autumn in your stride,
windows opening on your walk, your head

against the clouds. You are counting magpies
on the road, you are whistling without finding the tune.

One heel is pressing harder than the other,
your left hand is through your hair, adjusting your glasses.

From my room in another city, distant, windowless,
I am watching your progress, ensuring the magpies

only pass in twos, clearing your path
of every possible distraction: slow cyclists, escalators

out of operation, dogs on zebra crossings,
station bomb scares; counting the smallest parts

of every day, hairs on my arm, beat of blood
in the passage of my veins – much too breathless

for the ordinariness of clocks –
right till the moment you are here.

TEACHERS

The Geography teacher with a wooden leg
dictated notes about ox-bow river lakes,
subtracted marks if we changed the punctuation.
In English literature, we diverted the master
from *Julius Caesar* ('Describe the role of the mob in Act One')
by requesting his exploits in the Burmese War campaign.
He puffed on his pipe, selected manoeuvres –
we might be lucky, this could last for hours...

Mr Fawdrey taught Maths, but his passion was flying:
an RAF ramrod, he abandoned Venn diagrams
up on the blackboard, to squint out of the window,
scan low cloud for the faint hum of Boeings.
Reverend Challis covered RE *(Sir, what's a concubine?)*;
more dictation (colour-coded) for Chemistry, Biology,
and the inevitable milk bottles in Art still life,
one overgrown onion and some incongruous drapery.

Which only left History, and a passion for the teacher
that made my cock twitch, my heart pound in my ears.
I learned your dates like a religious mantra,
tattooed your battle plans across my skin. Naked in bed,
I recited the victories of the first Duke of Marlborough:
Ramilles, Oudenarde, Blenheim, Malplaquet.

FELLINI

Today I'd like to be in one of those over-the-top
1950s Fellini films.

I'd be monstrous, unblushing with huge, melon breasts
that you could rub your face in,
though I know you wouldn't;

or a mad uncle up a tree shouting *I want sex...*
with the whole family laughing and you down below
chomping on salami.

Or I'd be doing the old soft-shoe shuffle along the beach
at the straggling end of a wedding party –
sea up to my ankles, I wouldn't mind –

to the winsome tune of your dry-land accordion
from behind some chichi restaurant window;
or a paparazzo on a Vespa

shamelessly after your headline story,
wearing Marcello Mastroianni specs,
white raincoat flying,

while you snaked away up the Via Veneto –
glamorous in the backseat,
with not one turning look.

Or I'd be one big silhouette in the black and white light
shaking the chains around my rupturing he-man heart –
everything to give,

while you, the only other character left,
would be standing in the circus tent
wondering why you were there.

Then maybe the camera would pan round,
find you laughing then crying in spite of yourself –
as strangely big-hearted as all the rest.

FX

On emptying the BBC Spot Effects Store, Broadcasting House, 2003.
'Spot effects' (FX) is the name given to the actual physical objects which are used
by actors when recording radio dramas, rather than electronic sound effects.

The flipflop is FX 29, the dark brown teapot FX 324,
those inevitable coconut shells FX 561 –
though the ink here goes faint, is lost in brown wiry hair.

And beyond stand shelves of labelled cups and saucers,
handbags and suitcases, a stack of doors with noisily turning
                                     handles,
with knockers, letter boxes and one electric bell.

All wait on a summons – fill in a form, quote a number,
haul them out from soundless dust by the precision of your ear:
a tricycle in a corner is only waiting for asphalt,

bundles of umbrellas would flap out rain,
the coils of recording tape squashed in a bin liner
could soon skitter autumn leaves, just for the asking.

FX, FX, FX – held in the space of this long-eaved room,
labelled, sectioned, meaningless because mute,
waiting for the narrative to name their number.

These are not the story, never the story –
they're the world without words, at most a background hint.
But if the unthinkable should happen

and the story not appear, if the gaps in the words
should fill all the space,
then is the rest only silence, or unknowable noise?

FX 561 meets FX 324 meets...
Doors would open on a long foggy corridor
where that bell might ring and never ever stop,

where a flipflop and a sandal
might go walking for days, and those skittering
autumn leaves be always returning.

THE WATCH

You lost your watch in the sea one day.
It slipped off, was gulped by water, swallowed
in sand. You waved your blank wrist

at sunlight and never reclaimed its narrow band,
its luminous tick, its reminder. Then slowly your skin
turned to salt, your hair skeined white, your body

dropped deeper under water, scale-cold
to the touch, almost out of sight,
a different element – the claws of a cuttlefish

net-slipping days. Sometimes you'd surface
to watch me on the shore, walking past
the vast glass dome, glitter of traffic, cars in a line,

walking on the hands of that huge, shiny clock
with its numbers that glinted on the face of my sleep
as I turned in my bed to look out to sea.

I COME IN HERE

to find you on the brink of illness,
regularly tested, watchful: blue flesh under light,
a body untouchable behind glass,

or your back turned towards me
wading footprints up the dunes,
my eyes always following the line of sweat

down your dark blue shirt. I come in here,
jealous of all the thoughtless time that is gone,
in a variety of cities, and some of which

we might have met in – been easy,
without significance – so I have this bad dream
of perpetually walking past you in our pasts,

down a street, without one backward look.
I come in here, trying not to look too far forward,
trying to learn a way of walking in the sand –

the places where we stop, your dark shirt planted
like a flag – and how to look unswervingly
through glass and light.

THE MUSIC IN THE GARDEN

I leave the music playing in the house
as I move down to the rain-filled garden. Dark cello,
all dark brown wood, all echo – like the space

we make between walls and windows, arms
and eyes; like the strangeness of our connection

which sometimes seems as solid as this house,
sometimes as light as floatable as dust, the flap
of a curtain, water splashes on the bathroom mirror.

The music then the silence after, how it teases
at meanings of notes and string but leaves us no easy logic.

Yet down in the garden, among the spikes of rained-
on daisies, wilderness of mint and the fallen
pots of green tomato plants, I know it is playing

behind the black windows, the flowers in the jug
on the sill, the composure of stone. I bind up

broken stems, deadhead geraniums, pull snails off
the path, make order after rain, and I hear it
in my head, bending down I feel it, skin against my skin.

THE MISFITS

'One day, it happened, they were all there together:
Monroe, Clift, Gable and Miller'
– Elliott Erwitt, photographer, 1960.

Marilyn is mouthing kisses, centre frame –
décolletée, polkadots,
holding her breath for the sudden flash,
hair like a wig with scalloped curls unmoving;

Monty has his hand on his chin,
eyes staring hard at the camera lens –
out the other side and into nowhere,
his left foot turned inwards like a child unsure of walking;

while Clark is doing grimacing macho,
one cowboy boot anchored
on the crate behind Monroe, all five pearl buttons
neatly done up on his fringed shirt cuff.

At the back, the techs are arms crossed, waiting,
just wishing this guy would stop taking photos –
all time is money,
especially with a cast like this...

Miller's behind them, on top of a stepladder,
looking into distance
from behind those black framed specs,
a body too long for the camera pose.

The next frame, they're gone:
just desert and a pony's shadow galloping across the sand,
above it the line of a long, black lasso
trying and trying to catch that shadow.

PARCELS

This is the night for handing out parcels. Especially for you.
Unwrap the brown paper. There's a long, belted overcoat –

you will need it, for the waiting. And a cheap plastic whistle
with an imperfect pea, to call back the heads of unturning passersby.

There are books, magazines, ten cartons of cigarettes.
A station full of freezing waiting rooms. The polished floors

of selected museums: the Tate, the Prado, a late-night closing
at the National Gallery – all the walls hung with red-eyed saints.

There are songs to hum every second of the day: one you
                                        can't remember,
one that comes when you want it least, repeating and repeating.

There are light switches, dog barks, fireworks, car alarms, the starting
and stopping of the early morning milk float: everything that
                                        wakes you

when you want to sleep. There is one green-blue piece
of curly Venetian glass, bubble-wrapped with care so it won't
                                        get broken.

You can stamp on it now in your several pairs of shoes –
they're in the last parcel – the black, the brown, the buttoned and
                                        the laced.

You will need them all to pace the rainy streets in search of
                                        my window –
not this one nor that one, nor the one down the alley

reached by a broken staircase. There's no map for past wrongs,
and so little time to find me, so much brown paper, so much rain.

THE ROOM OF THE MODEL THEATRE SETS

For Sebastiano Romano

The end of the century. In your flat
Mimi is still dying again and again, Tosca mounting
the crenellated battlements.

                    Your Sicilian *pupi*
are dangling on the wall, the curl of their moustaches
liquorice-black, their mouths' bright lipstick

unsmudged by kisses. And of course the arrows,
drooping so elegant from your Saint Sebastian's flesh –
the little statue decorous under the lamplight –
white as a peach and beautiful, I remember,

so beautiful in the dark. In your designer's model theatre sets
all the paper cut-outs tremble on their sticks,
wave their tiny hands up to the light. You wake

with a start from your long insomnia, show me
the photos of the dead and dying: the razor blade cuts
that sting in the morning, the weight that makes
no space at all. You shout about graffiti on the Milan streets,

all along the train carriages unmoving in their tracks,
the sound of aerosol cans night after night –
            illegible smears in the unlovely morning.

PARIS DE NUIT

'There is no such thing as complete darkness'
– Notes from the Parisian photographer, Brassaï, 1932

I keep on walking through doorways, mirrors,
water house, slaughter house, night.

Twenty-four heavy glass negatives in my bag –
each needs a magnesium flash above the tripod,

each takes a long, slow moment.
The Canal Saint Martin is quiet tonight. Flash.

The butchers down by Les Halles flick blood on my lens
so I show their innocent eyes. Flash, flash.

Madame Suzy shifts a naked buttock against Monsieur's
serge-suited knee, she knows how he likes it –

wants the light off.
But there's enough in the dark for me:

a cigarette burning, a flash of her emerald ring.
Her head goes backwards, his eyes are in the mirror.

I keep on walking, wondering how to be part of fog
and not. How to peel back night a little longer.

How to keep on walking to where the chestnut flowers
are white as stars against the night. Flash.

Where there are cobbles, rain, the slick of his brillantined hair,
a mirror of black, black coffee. Flash.

Where the doorway waits with its thin silver line
holding in stair rods, keyholes, corners of rooms.

Where the night has one more shade of unrecorded black
for me to hold. One more flash before the light.

Till I wake in the morning inside my darkroom,
hang the *Do Not Disturb* sign upon the door, keep on walking.

ANGLEPOISE

Black hood, hanging head, narrow pool
of light – my eyes blinking in it.

Somewhere – in the kitchen down below –
there are the footsteps of my parents, radio news

or someone else's play coming through
the lines of the venetian blind.

Here, there is only that face beyond the glass,
beech tree leaves in its cheeks and hair,
its cold eyes watching nervous of everything,

learning to be somebody separate,
repeating the words – like yesterday's homework –
unheard beyond the window.

When I switch off the anglepoise, I wonder
if there's anyone there at all.

Or I wonder what it's like
to be waiting in the dark,
for the light inside to turn me on again.

TOAST

It is only carbon, us finding fire, a little taste
of warm crunched against the night.
But a small gap to coal, but one process more

to diamond. It is only us this evening
making comfort inside this room, drinking tea
in easy chairs, cut out against the lines

of orange wallpaper, a domestic interior
intimately repeated. Of scant significance.
It is just dark crumbs resting on your lips,

or the usual stars in our windowed London sky
burning their daily diamonds. The way
we forget sometimes to be amazed.

EXIT, PURSUED BY A BEAR

'A story has no beginning or end'– Graham Greene

Behind, the small ship, the man in a cape
with a broken lantern, the zigzags of light that catch at
my eye, make my nose grow wet.
But I begin here –

his footsteps moving, his smell among the leaves,
the fear in his blood that makes mine hot. He is lost,
lost again, shouting into the wind and soaked by rain.
His words are all endings, all Hail Marys and Amens.
But I begin now –

though I too had a before: a long brown story
that started in a cave, that pawed the earth and swallowed bees.
In front, is a baby bawling into the night, a glitter of gold
and a parchment scroll. I could eat the baby.
I could begin there –

but the man's a better feast. I watch him through the trees,
rub my fur against the dark. This is where he ends.
Tomorrow, he's a pile of bones in the sun. Tomorrow, that baby
will be sixteen years old. I could begin then –

10 poems, beginning and ending in a garden
in memory

THE GOOD MOMENT

It's a small thing, only a small thing,
but you will understand it – though you will want
to give it a name, a Latin name, as if erudition
will justify the miracle. If you don't know its name,
there will be a panic: you will start going through the alphabet,
as proof against senility. Or will heap the green encyclopedia
onto your lap, lick the corners of its pages, seek out
"shrubs, perennials, annuals with a blue flower".
But it's happiness all the same, even though we say it
with different words. And we sit together for a space,
watch the blue flower wave its bells - dark blue on light blue -
against the sun, catch their good moment. We know it won't last,
for you will be off with your secateurs making neatness,
clattering tea things, being my mother, and I will be playing
the unruly son, fidgetting with a key ring, thinking of lists
of undone things that I have to do elsewhere.

BLACKBERRIES

We come back with our stained hands
and sagging bag. It's something to do with the War
that makes her send us out to pick fruit
from the autumn hedgerows. A once-empty larder,
a too-small piece of garden, and she'll measure it again
and again, will never ever have enough.

Now we are off again – she waves us away at the door –
to stain our hands till the nails are blue-black,
the moons come bright white out from the cuticles.
She wants us to bring back all the fruit from the lane
and the abandoned brickfield and from behind
the recreation ground: her hands make the journey.

She wants us to pick and pick all afternoon
until there's not one blackberry left, all the briars
robbed and dangling as if lighter, carefree.
And a little bit of whatever she lost
will be regained, boiling in trickles of dark blue sugar,
saved and sweet, cooling slowly there in the pan.

SUITS

Yesterday I did the thing you always wanted me to do:
bought a suit, in fact I bought two.
One thick blue velvet corduroy,
the other mid-blue, in light-weight wool.
A summer bargain, halfway down Regent Street:
two suits for the price of one,
and they threw in the alterations
for my too thin waist, my too short leg.
And as I walked out into the lunchtime heat of Regent Street,
I thought I would ring you on the mobile
to make you so pleased
that your son had finally come to his senses
at the grand old age of forty-five,
given up the rebellion against collar and tie,
the Sunday suit, the interview suit, the wedding suit,
the anytime/anything event suit,
accompanied by your despairing look that said
"you can't go out wearing that".
I almost rang you again on the bus back from work,
practised my ironical rejoinders,
could hear the flush of proud "at last" in your voice.
But I had somewhere to rush to,
then was trying to send an email
with a recalcitrant attachment,
then left in a hurry to go out for a meal.
Then they rang me in the morning
to say you had died in the night,
so you would never know about my two blue suits
nor all the other things
I never did find time to tell you.

THE VISIT

The person you were before I ever knew you,
quite separate and young, nothing yet to do with me,
came to my room in the middle of the day.
There was a train you had to catch, you needed a book,
a particular poem – *Is there anybody there?* it began.
Could I help you by remembering the title, the author,
point you to the volume, its slim red cover.
I wanted to keep you talking so pretended I had it
on one of these shelves. I observed your directness,
light in your eye, your composure of readiness,
the almost laughter rising in your throat,
and I scanned your face for a trace of me,
for a beat of knowing before connection.
But you twisted on your chair, you couldn't wait –
there was a war on, you know, a man in the Signals
back from Egypt; children behind desks
staring at the blackboard, waiting for your teacher's chalk
to make the words ("round and up and down and flick").
There was a red satin dress to be cut and sewn,
the hat with paper flowers saying *Roses of Picardie*;
bulbs to be planted along the crazy-paving path;
a holiday in Dorset, two funerals in Shropshire –
the hated father, then the mother with tea tray
toppling down the stair after him...
such a lot to do before the babies came.
You gave me your hand inside its smooth cotton glove.
If I remembered the poem I'd be sure to let you know.
You could hear the rhythm, just the words
that escaped you. *Oh yes,* I said, *I'd be certain to do so,*
holding the hand of the unknown you –
as you waited there, my almost mother,
in the frame of the doorway – then letting you go.

WAS

I find myself marvelling
how easily I have done it,
flicked a tiny switch

and made the language work,
is becomes *was*,
time makes sense of time.

More verbs come later –
half-hidden stepping stones
I leap across the water;

or like those fence poles that flicker
at the edge of the road
where I feel the car leaning

to the space beside my eye,
then I resist, correct the wheel,
keep on going.

WEEDS

The ground elder now invades the garden,
which she would hate.
And shepherd's purse, dandelion, rosebay willow herb,
a sprawl of bramble...

they follow soon after.
Wasteground weeds she'd have said with a sniff.
But now they all come,
fill the space, riot with growth in this rainy spring.

I let them come –
and the spiders in the bathroom –
for her over-trim garden was never to my taste.
Let them come, let them grow: their nodding pink heads,
tough yellow stars, vigorous suckers scaling the wall,
their long white taproots
pushing deep down beneath the earth.
I let them soften the edges,
scratch and blur the borders,

making it a different garden from the one she knew,
as if I were saying to her "Now you relax,
now at last
you give way.

We can walk the garden of wild, uncertain things
and have no fear of what we might find.
We can stand here in the night
and feel it grow...

the fibrous, risky air,
the sound – when you listen –
of more and more."

ORPHEUS WITH FLOWERS
AND A KITCHEN UTENSIL

For Neil Drury

I like your paintings
and their incongruous titles.
Take this one – its purple face
with eyes half-perceptible,
this writing you tell me
to read backwards in a mirror;
these mixed-season flowers –
swollen tulips, gypsophila, scentless jasmine –
curving to the right out of the picture,
as if a hand had tilted the vase,
had tired of flat surfaces
and sense of order;
then this kitchen utensil, an old used ladle,
lying sideways under the face,
scooping up shadow and holding it there
at the corner of the picture,
this ordinary life –
yes, even Orpheus
had to go back to a house,
a room, a window,
had to watch her go, then –
hours, days passing,
a mirror turning black then white –
had to take down the ladle
from the kitchen wall,
decide what to eat, how to go on.

AT THE NEWEL POST

We are always talking, talking about them,
wanting them gone –
out of our adolescent bedrooms,
out of their house, away.
In our holidays from them,
we grow our hair and break their furniture,
leave stains on the carpet,
talk louder and louder into the mirror
as if to make our words believable.

When they're finally gone –
leaving us with cupboards
full of too familiar clothing and the smell of alone –
we carry on talking, talking about them
till we suddenly find
we have slipped inside the skin of them,
the set of their bones,
their way of sounding.

So I find myself here,
hand on the newel post at the top of the stair –
the rightness in my palm
of its smooth wooden egg –
facing the day with just my mother's gaze;
or making her lists of daily tasks
with that click of her tongue –
half the tasks written there,
though already done – to drive me through hours
with unstoppable ardour.

Or increasingly, like my father,
I sit under the lamplight, the still, white pool of it,
reading and not reading into the night,
talking to myself
but only half-listening.

MINT

I am chopping up the last mint of summer.
It's a ritual goodbye –

goes with sandals, bare legs, shorts, and suntan lotion,
alfresco dinners and the candles burning
to a waxen stump
among the garden leaves.

Last mint on my fingers now,
the scent of it pushed through my hair
when I lift my hand
from a finishing touch to dinner.

Last ritual in a ritual,
and everything I've ever learned
seems to come back
to the comfort and confines of cycles such as these –

how I am balanced on the last, sharp edges
of that pepper scent which I want to be everywhere,
holding it close
with every intensity I shall ever have,

and how I forget it, in the snow-filled silence
of my three-month-hence garden,
so I wonder to myself

Did I ever eat mint? Did I ever crush it on the circle
of this wide blue plate? Did I ever crave a summer,
long and green and full of this?

The mystery is
what we do with loves even as small as this –
how we learn to live with them,
how we learn to forget.

BONFIRES

Come back in bonfires
at the turn of the year
when the sky is dark blue,

the houses sealed up
against the cold.
Come back in that flare

of piled-on warm,
a forgotten red
which rushes right in

at the heart.
We are one in a ring.
We are watchful eyes

and extended hands.
We are stood cut out
against the night.

You are piled high
burning in this moment,
a practical heaping

of leaves and lives.
Come back in bonfires
at the turn of the year.

Acknowledgements

Acknowledgements are due to the Editors of the following magazines and anthologies where some of these poems first appeared: *Ambit, Tabla, Boomerang, Magma, The Interpreter's House, Frogmore Papers, The Waterlog, Oxford Poetry, Chroma, Exit 21, Housman Poetry Prize Anthology*

'On Flying to meet Your New Lover' was commended in the Housman Prize competition.

'The Visit' was commended in the Myeloma/Interpreter's House competition.

'Tortoise' was commended in the Leicester Open Poetry competition.

'Amsterdam' won 2nd prize in the Torbay Poetry Competition.

With special thanks to the Thursday Group, to Jo Roach for the poem behind 'I Come From', and to Jane Duran for her unfailing inspiration and support.